Ever After:

Tips for Parenting Your Child the Way You Want To

By

Dr. Angela D. Martin

Table of contents

Introduction

What makes good parent?

Someone who always makes an effort to act in their child's best interest is the definition of a good parent.

It is not simply a parent's actions that characterize them as a good parent; the parent's intentions are

It is not simply a parent's actions that characterize them as good parents; the parent's intentions are just as important.

A good parent should not be an ideal example for their children. No one is completely faultless. Nobody's flawless, not even kids... We must keep this in mind when we set our goals.

Being a good parent does not require reaching a level of perfection. However, this does not imply that we shouldn't try to achieve that aim. First and first, we should hold ourselves to high standards, and only then can we expect them of our children. We are significant examples for children to follow since they look up to us.

A child's connection with his or her parents or primary caregiver is the one that will have the most influence on the development of the kid. A healthy connection between a parent and their kid is the primary vehicle via which a youngster acquires knowledge about the world. Kids look to their parents to determine whether or not they are loved, protected, and safe as they go through the development and maturation process. Additionally, it serves as the basis for constructing their future connections.

You may cultivate a healthy parent-child connection by being fully present with your kid, devoting high-quality time to the two of you, and providing an atmosphere where they feel at ease exploring the world around them. No magic instruction manual or fool proof method can successfully get you through this relationship, and you should prepare for challenges. Your child's development will undoubtedly be positively impacted, though, if you continue to strengthen the bond between the two of you.

Continue reading for eight effective strategies for good parenting that will assist you in building a stronger bond with your child:

A good parent doesn't need to be an ideal example for their children. Everyone has flaws and imperfections. Additionally, there is no such thing as a flawless kid... We must keep this in mind when we establish our goals and standards.

Parenting successfully does not require striving for perfection in any aspect of the role. However, this does not imply that we shouldn't continue to strive towards achieving that objective. First and first, we should hold ourselves to rigorous standards, and only then can we expect them of our children. They look up to us as significant models, which is an honour.

A child's connection with his or her parents or primary caregiver is the most significant and formative of all the relationships they will have throughout their lifetime. A healthy connection between a parent and their kid is the primary vehicle via which a youngster acquires knowledge about the world. Children look to their parents to assess whether or not they are loved, protected, and safe as they go through the development and maturation process. Additionally, it serves as the basis for constructing their future connections.

You may cultivate a healthy parent-child connection by being fully present with your kid, devoting high-quality time to the two of you, and providing an atmosphere where they feel at ease exploring the world around them. No magic instruction manual or fool proof method can successfully get you through this relationship, and you should prepare for challenges. Your child's development will undoubtedly be positively impacted, though, if you continue to strengthen the bond between the two of you.

Continue reading for eight effective strategies for good parenting that will assist you in building a stronger bond with your child:

Chapter 1

Decent within

I believe that you and your children are both amazing individuals because of how you raise them.

When I say that all of us are "decent inside," I mean that we are sympathetic, loving, and giving individuals.

Kindness from the inside serves as the overarching conceptual framework for all of my work.

Because I believe that on the inside, both children and their parents are good individuals, I am able to ask "why" when either displays poor behavior.

Because of my natural curiosity, I can design and implement strategies and frameworks that are effective in bringing about change.

The connection kids have with their parents, or another main caregiver is the one that has the most impact on their development throughout their lifetime.

A close connection between parents and their children benefits a child's education about the world in which they live.

As children grow and evolve, they look to their parents to find out if they are loved, secure, and safe.

On top of this foundation, they will build the connections that they will use in the future.

You may be able to build a solid bond with your kid if you are there with them, if you spend quality time with them, and if you create an atmosphere in which they feel comfortable venturing out on their own and exploring.

There is no secret recipe or guaranteed method for developing a satisfying romantic connection, and it is quite likely that you may face some difficulties along the road. However, if you continue to focus on deepening your relationship with your kid or children, they will experience an increase in happiness in their development. There is nothing in this book that gives any indication that we need to behave any differently than we would if we let irritation and wrath dictate the decisions that we made.

Chapter 2

Character is a window

Contemplate Your Very Own Formative Years.

Many of us want to raise our children differently from our own parents. Certain people, even those who had a healthy and happy childhood and a wonderful upbringing, would desire to alter some parts of the way they were brought up.

However, when we open our lips, we quite often use the same phrases that our own parents used.

The first step in comprehending the motivations behind our parenting styles is to go back to our own formative years. Make a note of the things that you would want to alter, and consider how you may approach this situation in the real world differently. You should make an effort to be more conscious and adjust your behavior the next time such problems arise.

If, at first, you are unsuccessful, you should not give up. To bring about a deliberate shift in one's approach to the upbringing one's children requires practice and plenty of it.

Positive parenting should include both kindness and firmness.

About 100 billion neurons are present in the brains of newborn babies, but the connections between these neurons are few. These connections give rise to our ideas, motivate our activities, contribute to developing our personalities, and, in the end, establish who we are. Our life experiences contribute to the formation, consolidation, and "sculpting" of these identities.

In the early years, it is important to provide your kid with a pleasant connection within the family. They will then be able to benefit from pleasant experiences for themselves and share those benefits with others.

However, if you expose your kid to unpleasant events, they won't have the growth that is essential for them to be successful in life.

Sing that ridiculous tune. Have a tickle-fest of epic proportions. You should go to the park. Laugh together with your little one. Give them the kind of attention they want. Bear witness to and accompany them through their emotional outburst. Together, with a constructive mindset, we can find a solution to the issue.

Not only do these enjoyable activities foster the development of healthy synaptic connections in your kid's brain, but they also contribute to the formation of memories of you that your child will carry with them throughout their whole lives.

When it comes to matters of discipline, it may be challenging to have a good attitude, particularly when one is dealing with behavioural issues. However, this may be accomplished via the use of constructive discipline rather than severe punishment.

To be a successful parent, you need to instil in your kid a sense of what is morally acceptable and unacceptable in their behaviour.

The key to strong discipline is establishing limitations and being consistent with those restrictions. When you establish rules and enforce them, do it in a manner that is both courteous and forceful. Concentrate on discovering why the youngster is behaving in such an unacceptable manner. Instead of being penalized for things that happened in the past, make this experience an opportunity for them to learn something useful for the future in a constructive manner.

Chapter 3

Establishing connections and addressing actions

Smile

Performing this small experiment tends to make children anxious, but it also alters the atmosphere in the house. Simply choose a few times during the day when you will consciously make an effort to smile more.

It was wonderful what she observed, and she really had feedback from her children that it made a difference for them to grin more. One of the mothers in my coaching group did this with her children, and it was incredible what she saw as a result.

Choose to take pleasure in every step.

Hmm. The levels, you say? And every stage of development because there are fun things to enjoy when your kids are infants, when they're toddlers, when they're young children, when they're older children, even when they're teenagers, there are things that you can enjoy on. The part that I want to emphasize here is every stage of development because there are fun things to enjoy when your kids are infants, when they're toddlers when they're young children, when they're older children The candidate of choice is you as parent. You have a choice; that much is certain. Enjoying yourself at this stage should be a conscious decision. If your kid is already there, you should tell them, "Do you view it as a choice?" It is not, despite the fact that it is quite simple to fall into that trap. Therefore, you should make an effort to achieve that goal.

Instead of concentrating on the result, you should pay attention to the relationship.

You should know it, in my opinion. Often we go so deep merely hooked to. I want my kid to have these characteristics, to behave in this way, to like these activities, and so on. Just give attention to the connection between us. When I'm dealing with the kid, I should be thinking about how the youngster feels about himself, right? One of the ways that we expressed this was not too long ago within the context of a family in which you are aware that I was promoting the growth of certain family ties prior to the establishment of family norms. We are still going to follow the regulations, but the focus now is on strengthening our connection. The attention needs to be directed in that direction.

Learn how to deal with the consequences.

Now, what exactly do you mean when you talk about the consequences? Essentially repercussions for disobedience or repercussions for the things that you're working on with your children? For better behaviour, we need to become good at consequences; a lot of parents run into frustrations because they aren't sure what type of consequences to apply to their children. On, for better behaviour, we got to get excellent at consequences. I will not go into all of the specifics of that at this time due to the nature of this particular situation. I can provide you with further information on that topic, but first, you need to become proficient in it. This is a collection of skills that parents should have. So be ready to put in some effort, get ready to put in some practice, and receive the assistance you need to become skilled at dealing with the repercussions of your actions. Mentioning these resources will, therefore, provide you with a wealth of suggestions for how to personalize the consequences in order to motivate improved behaviour.

Separate yourself from the results.

This is a challenging question. This is a tremendously challenging question since we often believe that the success of our parenting is measured by the actions or consequences of our children. And in all honesty, we are working towards improving the behaviour, aren't we? When we wish to separate ourselves from the result, doing it in this manner is rather contradictory. Despite the fact that we are acting in this manner with the hopes of achieving more favourable results. I'm going to put in a psychological justification for this as well since someone needs to have an emotional investment in the result, right? And if it is you, your child is not the one in trouble. Yeah. Additionally, they are quite effective in the way that they think. So this is what your children are always contemplating. Hmm. Should I be concerned about this, or should I allow someone else to be concerned about it? If I let somebody else be concerned, it will be simpler for me. If my mother is concerned about this, I'm going to leave it up to her and concentrate on my own concerns.

Stage, not age.

Put this in writing someplace, and give some thought to what you've just read. The term "stage" refers to a child's current point in the progression of their moral development; children of varying ages and stages may coexist. You may have a younger kid who is extremely mature, makes solid judgments constantly in collaboration, and obeys, while you may have a teenager who behaves in the complete opposite manner. It just kind of changed all of the way that this man approached his parenting now because he understood that it was the stage, not age. You know, I remember in a seminar that we did once when a parent the lightbulb went on, they have the parent of a child with special needs and all of a sudden was like ding, oh, she's at this stage just because she's this, all does not mean, she's on this stage and it just kind of changed the way that Right. Effective for you, and the progression of events is a factor that determines how we operate. Our discipline, right? I would want to know what type of remarks there are and what time it is. Therefore, the fact that your kid is requesting a phone at the age of 13 or that your child is asking for some independence at the age of 17 does not necessarily imply that they are mature enough for it yet. This has to do with the stage of moral growth that they are now in. Stage, not age, should be written down someplace, so simply do that. In addition to that, it will provide you with access to some further resources that will assist you in comprehending the significance of what that statement implies.

Your children deserve your love.

That is a fantastic method of good parenting, and it really does assist bring about improved behaviour. As a parent, it is your responsibility to do so. How does loving them fit into your job description? Whatever the case may be. And although if this is something that most parents already do without thinking, we still need to recognize that it is one of the laws of healthy parenting. You are aware of how significant the role of love plays in successful parenting, so this one probably did not come as a surprise to you either. Take note that there are still two rules remaining, despite the fact that it is your primary responsibility as a parent to love your children regardless of what they do.

Remember to look out for the team.

Keep in mind that you are going to be responsible for the development of this team. It may be you and your spouse; it could be you as a parent, or it could be you as a close friend. All of these scenarios are possible. I really have no idea. However, you are responsible for taking care of that team. It's been said that "it takes a village to raise a kid," but if you ask me, I'd say, "it requires a team at the very least when the team is strong." There's an ancient proverb that says, "it takes a village to raise a child." The youngster has the greatest potential for achievement. Because of this, we are making this point. Let me give you a brief example. When parents get a babysitter or pay someone else to watch their children for a short period of time so that they can attend to the needs of the team or relationship, they may experience feelings of guilt. However, despite these feelings, this is one of the most important gifts that parents can give their children in order to strengthen the team. It makes their environment more stable and secure, as well as more predictable, which is beneficial to them.

I worked anywhere between ten and seventeen years, completing child custody assessments for the court when I was resentful, furious, and going through a divorce. People were at a loss on how to divide up their children fairly. There are still options available to you despite the fact that the team has broken up. If you are part of a family that consists of different households, all you need to do is work toward strengthening that team and providing those children with the consistency and security they need. What else could possibly be than loving your children and looking out for the well-being of the team?

Today marks the end of the countdown, which brings us to the last phase.

Putting yourself first in everything you do.

When you consider it from the perspective of a parent, doesn't it seem completely counterintuitive? taking care of yourself, but it's the number one guideline of good parenting. Taking care of yourself.

If you're not in the running, then you definitely aren't in the running. And your children are counting on you. Additionally, there is one more facet to this that I don't go into a lot of detail about in this specific book, yet, this facet is essential.

If you aren't taking care of yourself, who is? If the response is your children, this dynamic is backward and will have a negative impact on their development. They should not be placed in a situation where they are required to look after their parents until much later in life, at the earliest. When the time comes, you become an elderly person, and they have a responsibility to care for you in that regard. I am referring to the time when they were young and when they were going through these key developmental phases. In my professional work, I have seen situations in which children are required to take care of their parents due to addiction or other impairments or issues. I want you to be the most wonderful example of a parent that your kid could ever have. That implies you have the responsibility of looking for yourself. This is the first and most important rule, Mama bomb. You won't need any help with this. You have access to an enormous amount of information.

Chapter 4

Fighting among siblings

Many of my readers have asked me to address the problem of fighting among siblings, and I've had a lot of requests to do so. How do you tackle issues like that? Let's get started on it right now.

Let's take a step back since the fact that your children are fighting with one another may have something to do with the norms and traditions that have been established in your home from the very beginning. You may get a head start on fostering a culture of respect from the very beginning. This is important to do since fostering a culture of respect is incredibly challenging, but it is necessary. I have a memory of receiving a letter from my brother at one point when his daughter was quite young—I believe she was only three or so—and in the letter, he stated that he respected her a great deal, which struck me as very odd at the time. I remember thinking that my brother's daughter was quite mature for her age. Before today, I had never given much attention to the concept of an older person showing proper deference to a younger youngster. Interesting. That right there is a culture. And I've written in the past on the book about family rules, and you know that they all revolve around showing respect for one another, right? Yeah. Should I take a moment to go back and look at them before we continue?

Now for the very first step,

Respect both yourself and the people around you.

Do you have any idea what this regulation may possibly have to do with the constant fighting that goes on among siblings? It is, in fact, a regulation. Home and inside the family are where you may learn to respect yourself as well as others. Respect yourself because a lot of the time, when we get into arguments with other people, it isn't really about them as much as it is about us. I know what you're saying, and I love the commercials, but respect yourself because, a lot of the time, it is about you. If we are feeling uneasy or not entirely content with something, we are more likely to initiate a quarrel. This is a really accurate statement. Yes. Right. It's possible that this is going on behind your back with your children. The regulation is as stated. First and foremost, have respect for yourself and others.

Let's go on to the second step, shall we?

Property specification

This has a great deal more to do with the items and belongings you have than it does with the yard that your neighbours have. He never stopped quizzing children on the meaning of the word "property." It belongs to my next-door neighbours. You know that your mom is constantly harping on the fact that you shouldn't go on their property, right? Therefore, it is the yard, but it also includes your assets and how you treat things, and it is related to how things are handled. When siblings argue, it's often about things, but sometimes it's just about nothing. Also, if they're not treating it with respect there, that's a problem.

Their own things, toys, or an alternative take on it. It's exciting to have to put an end to the battle that the kids have begun, but at the same time, it's necessary. Instead of getting into your mean, you could go into the, well yeah, the appropriate rule for our family is to respect property! This means that you can't take your brother's item without asking him first because that's not respectful, and you also can't throw it because that's not respectful either.

Wherever are you aware of that, right? It is important to treat the thing with respect, both in terms of the item itself and where it is stored, and to refrain from making unauthorized use of the item.

In addition, moving on to the next level, which is;

Sharing in an appropriate manner.

We have a problem with our sense of priority if, for whatever reason, we place objects as a higher priority than people. Therefore, showing respect for property is ingrained in the ethos of the family.

And then the fourth one, which is also related to respect in the same manner that I've said in the past, is that.

Comply and be submissive.

Right? Which has anything to do with showing respect for authority at the moment. This is a bit of a conundrum because you use the term "authority," but at the same time, you want the youngsters to respect you.

To introduce the element of cooperation, no Bay should be used with their siblings. Even while there is not yet a clearly defined authority or a hierarchical right in place, there is still some degree of authority in it. It is in everyone's best interest to work together. Hmm. There is little distinction between collaborating and obeying, and the way that I explain this concept to children is that you should collaborate with whomever it is that is requesting you to carry out a task. That is correct, and it makes sense, regardless of whether or not they are in a position of control over you. Therefore, if your younger sister is in need of some assistance with anything, or if she has requested you for some assistance, or if she wants you to share something with her right now, you should cooperate with her. After all, obeying has something to do with authority, right? The one had a somewhat different take on things, as did that one. And I believe that it is of the utmost significance.

Again, I've discussed this topic in other books; it's important to understand the distinction between simply caving into some of the authority and obeying when they're asking for something reasonable, and that's right. It is beneficial for children to have a clear understanding of who they should obey.

Now let's make the assumption that you, as the child's parent, are asking them to do something that is morally sound and in line with common sense. Who else has authority over this child? There is a diverse collection of individuals. Isn't it possible that it's the teacher from the school? Perhaps a member of law enforcement or a judge.

Perhaps it's a neighbour who is in need of something, or perhaps it's their property that's being discussed, in which case the conversation pertains to the cooperative again. Because cooperating with them is the appropriate action to take, even if they lack direct authority. So long as they continue to inquire about it. It is something that is reasonable and correct at the same time. You seem to be helping the kids with their fighting, which is important because this is the culture that we want to establish for our family. You're going to do everything you can to ensure that you have the culture and the rules established in your own organization, right?

This is the groundwork, this is the basis for everything else that you are going to ask your children to do now in relation to the fighting, and it is at the heart of the matter. Okay. Now that you have some children fighting, how can you get them to stop fighting with each other, and what should we do next? The very next action plan is;

Recognize what developmental stage your child is currently in.

Indeed, you are absolutely correct. You need to have a firm knowledge and understanding of the stage that your child is currently in. While they're acting out, they're acting out while they're acting out. Whatever it may be, is that correct? In order for you to be able to use the appropriate consequence with them. So, it's the three C's, whether you're going to go with "consequences communication or consultation," so right now, try and remember these three stages. If you don't remember the three stages, I'm not going into it.

Understanding their stage of moral reasoning and development is going to guide how you approach it as a parent. So here's a quick example. Let's say that two of the kids are fighting with each other, and you intervene to stop the fight; right, you guys, stop! Wait, can I interject something? Besides the two kids fighting, they're kind of acting in stage 4. remember cooperation? Yes, it is the one you get passed out of stage 1 and Stage 2. So right now, they're acting stage one, but as soon as you start talking to them, they might not; they might flip right into Stage 2 with you. Yeah, so you, yeah, if they decide to cooperate, so be aware that even though their behaviour right at the moment is the stage, One. They might come as soon as your kind of step in and start intervening, and they might be able to swap it and go right back into Stage 2 with your right situation, at which point it is going to be a lot easier. That's how you're going to be able to tell what stage they're on. Because if they respond, they start to cooperate with you as you're intervening to break up the fight. Then they're in stage 2.

So let me ask you this, what if you've got to kiss, fighting, obviously, and child A is ready to move into Stage 4 and cooperate with you, but child B is Just fighting like crazy?

Still, I had a situation like that in my family a long time ago, and I guess what I'm saying is the way that you're dealing with sibling rivalry and the way that they're fighting might not be the same for each child.

Exactly, Child A is going to stay in stage one, you're going to use a consequence, and if child B is willing to come and meet you with cooperation, then you're going to change the type of you'll still use consequences, but there will be a different kind of consequence if they're willing to cooperate with you.

It could be for a stage one child. For example, you might restrict access to something that they really enjoy having access to my big game system. It might be the electronics in the home. It might be access to certain areas in your home, right? You can enforce that 100%. Now, with the other child cooperating with you, you're going to have some communication. I mentioned that we use consequences and stage one, communication. Plus, consequences at stage 2, but the consequences shift because now there's a kind that can require cooperation, and then consultation is stage 3.

I'm going to talk about that because usually, you're not fighting. That's the case. That's not why you're reading the book. So with that stage to the child, you'll have a conversation. You might say something like, let's work together on getting along and making sure that we follow rule number one, which is to respect. Selves and others. That means we don't fight with each other, and your child will be like, I know. Okay, I need to do better, and they're going along with you right now.

Do you have a consequence? Yeah, you might. And that consequence might be a writing assignment, a little essay about how to treat people. It might be that they get to do an extra chore. Some active service for that sibling, the one that they were fighting with, you can see that those kinds of consequences require cooperation. So I only use them as stage one kids. If your child is not cooperating, it has to be something that you control 100%, that you can enforce whether they want you to or not, right? Okay. You know, you mentioned a service or something like that kind of pulls us into another part when you're setting up the family culture. Yeah, you know, I talked about the three rules and other cultural aspects you might want to set up in your family somehow is,

Service among the children

Serving each other. This is to each other and one of the reasons that happen, you know, when you're born into a family, your siblings and you all know this unless you're an only child, you don't always pick your siblings, you would necessarily pick their personality to be your best friend, right? You know, it's just kind of happenstance. So there are some personalities that you have to learn on how to get along with each other. You have to learn how to like them. And one of the most effective methods to acquire knowledge on how to like and love somebody is by serving them.

That is true. So you can make some fun games and activities or fighting isn't happening to try to help the siblings get to know one another better and to like each other better.

I like what I write about making this part of the family culture.

You can also integrate this as a consequence for a stage 2 child, someone who's already cooperating with you, and its kind of fun to make this a challenge from time to time, just as part of your family culture, where you might have Secret Service. Okay, no. That sounds like somebody who protects the President, right? But it's also you secretly do acts of service for someone that you've drawn out in the family meeting or something like that, but you can even change or add it to your family culture. Like you've got a little three-year-old, maybe that's oftentimes in stage 1 because that's their age, right? And you say, hey, we ought to do ABC for so-and-so because we know that makes them happy and that they really like it. Let's go do that. And so you're doing it at a time when there's no emotional charge, right?

Chapter 5

Calming rage

There are moments in each of our lives when rage just takes control of our minds. Where does it leave our young ones? What can you do to help a youngster who is having trouble controlling their anger when their brains are even more immature? As they go through the many phases of childhood development, it is totally natural for children to go through the emotion of rage. You'll notice, for instance, that your children are going to feel frustrated from time to time. This is something that's very normal. They are engaging in brand-new developmental activities, which is to be expected; hence this behaviour is considered normal. This became very apparent to me in regard to my eldest daughter when she was going through a new phase in her life when she was learning how to walk. For example, while she was learning to communicate before she achieved these major developmental milestones, she would experience periods of frustration. This happened very often. And I believe the reason for that is that her tiny brain was thinking, well, I really want to do that thing, but her body wasn't there to assist her in doing it yet, and that generates frustration, and frustration can easily lead to anger and outbursts of rage.

It is normal for your kids to experience anger; it is normal for you, too, when big things are happening in your life; however, it is more normal for you to be more emotionally sensitive; let's turn that into a positive and make sure that we use empathy to connect with our children. Of course, anger; be aware of this; this is a normal part of the developmental process that your children are going through. In addition to the fact that this is perfectly natural, there are also instances when it may go a bit out of hand, and our children can learn to regulate it.

Their rage in a more acceptable manner. Where do anger and resentment often begin? A good many of my customers have learned from me that anger is a secondary emotion. And what I mean by that is that often there is another feeling that comes before the anger. I mentioned frustration before, and it comes right before the fury. For instance, this is one of the most prevalent ones, but there are also other things like loss, grief, or disappointment, and these are the things that often come first since it is more difficult to choose what to do with them. Anger is a kind of feeling, and it's rather straightforward to find out how to deal with it.

Okay, so we are all aware of how to deal with our anger, right? The emotional education that we provide for our children may offer them the words and descriptions of these other more fundamental teachings, which might be of assistance to them. We act out, and it's a really active sort of feeling. So doing stuff like that will be one of the things that we want to do when our children become older. Give them the language to articulate the feelings that they are experiencing by describing them to them.

Here are five concrete suggestions that might be of assistance when dealing with children who are throwing angry tantrums.

The first, and most likely most significant among them, is that.

Exemplify acceptable conduct.

It is never inappropriate for someone to feel

whatever it is that they are experiencing.

Therefore, it is not inappropriate to feel the wrath. As a parent, you may address that feeling in suitable and incorrect ways, depending on how you look at it. It is necessary for us to demonstrate the correct way to communicate such sentiments. Therefore, it is essential to maintain your composure. Have some confidence. Also, the sensations your kid now has will likely shift. As a psychologist, have you observed this phenomenon? This topic keeps coming up for me, which seems sensible, given that people are experiencing such strong emotions, right? Take careful notice of the shift in how you're feeling. Consider the following scenario: you are inside your house or workplace, and you look out the window to see thunderclouds and lightning. You can tell that a storm is developing, can't you? And you suddenly realize that the windows of your car are all wide open. What do you do? You walk outside, and you raise your fists to me? No, it won't do anything useful at all. You just exit the building and check to see that all of the windows on your car are rolled up, right? When your kid first begins to have a tiny storm for you to deal with, you should always try to ride out the storm and let it pass. Don't begin with me because it's just going to grow worse, it won't put an end to the storm, and this isn't something that can be quelled. The storm made it necessary to batten down the hatches and shut them and board up the windows. If there is a significant storm, whether or not the storm is going to pass, once the storm has passed, then we can conduct the necessary clean-up. If you have to, the storm is going to pass. Remember that these feelings seldom last, and keep this in mind while your kid works through his or her anger. When I go back, I can see one of my co-workers having a conversation with his little nephew when they were riding in the backseat of a vehicle. My co-worker just turned around while he was throwing a fit; he was throwing such a fit that you wouldn't believe it. He was having a tantrum like you wouldn't believe. I was quite amazed by the way that he dealt with the situation that he turned around. And he says it like way, Jean, son, friend. How much longer do you need, considering that this child is, I don't know, maybe five years old at this point, and he's free to go? He is sitting comfortably in his car seat pitch. Shit. Oh, it stings. His dad asks him? How much time do you require? Thirty minutes He said. And he claims that everything's okay, that he just turned around, and that it wasn't even two minutes. It was probably another twenty seconds before he came down and said that he was finished.

This is a common activity for children. This paints a picture of what I'm talking about, even if that's probably not the case. You keep your composure, all right? Prepare yourself to ride out the storm for two minutes or whatever long it lasts. It's going to take some storms, but they always pass, so just keep your cool. It will assist the storm in passing more quickly and, as a result, get it.

Now, let's go on to the second piece of advice, which is something that I will say.

The right actions to take in order to establish the parameters of safety.

There will be occasions when your child's rage is so out of control that they pose a risk of injuring themselves or someone else. In these instances, it is imperative that you take the necessary precautions to establish clear boundaries for the sake of their safety. Sometimes this requires you to exercise control, but you must proceed with caution in this area since you should never go over the line into abusive behaviour. But when it comes to a little kid, for instance, who is wriggling all about her and seems to be getting ready to, you know, damage themselves in some way or go out into the street or anything, this may be dangerous. It is acceptable to behave safely. Let's put some limits on those immature children. You can really hold them without putting any pressure on them, but you should be cautious. Be prudent and prudent in this matter; yet, it is acceptable to establish suitable limitations for them so that they do not do harm to themselves or others. Talk to an expert who can provide you with some direction if you feel like you need assistance with this.

The third piece of advice,

Create a channel of communication.

This is the point when the wrath, the overwhelming sensation, and the anger that they are now experiencing may be converted back into proper speech. Again, it is essential to demonstrate appropriate behaviour to your children in this regard. One way that you can accomplish this is by remaining calm and saying something to the effect of "when you can talk to me in the same kind of voice that I'm using with, we will be able to solve this." By doing this, you are modelling the idea that when you can talk to me the way that I'm talking to you, we can solve this problem. This then gives them an opportunity for a question and answer session, which will help us get back into communication mode, and you can reassure them. Also, in relation to what we've already covered, namely that they're never wrong about their feelings, use empathy. Make a statement that falls within these parameters. As soon as the communication is re-established, we can move on to the fourth piece of advice. Which is;

To give adequate alternatives.

What options do they have for dealing with the sensations that they are experiencing? Now, before we continue, I feel obligated to admit that I'm not a great fan of some of the conventional folklore that goes around saying, "Oh, go punch a pillow," right? And the fact that it pushes them to have an aggressive outlet for the sentiments that they are experiencing is one of the reasons why I have an issue with it. I'm considerably larger. The proponent of proper communication usage. Words. In point of fact, this is going to be the alternative that we teach our children to utilize when we tell them to use their words whenever they are feeling annoyed and agitated. Consequently, you switch gears and focus on communication. You then proceed to remark something along the lines of "I know you were extremely upset, right," don't you? And you're providing your kid with this empathetic support even if your youngster is being really unhappy about whatever it is. When we're frustrated, we vent our feelings via the words that we say. What are a few examples of words? That is a topic that might be discussed by you. The development of your kid has a significant role in how we would approach this situation. For instance, if we have a preverbal child, like a young toddler, we will approach this situation quite differently than we would with an older child who is able to utilize speech. So what I'm talking about here are children who are just on the edge of moving from the Aric stage 1 to the Stage 2 category.

I'm sure there's one on good parenting that will assist in shedding some light on what I mean when I speak about those different phases of development in children.

We are encouraging our children to utilize an alternative that is suitable, and we particularly and principally want them to use their own language. Words. What more could they possibly do to upset you when you're already feeling this way? It's important to take deep breaths. Okay, got it. Now, about breathing, I've used this technique with a great number of children, and we've had to practice it while the children were in a calm state. Okay? Because when people are angry, they are really not thinking and are operating from a totally different portion of their brain than when they are not upset. Therefore, during times when they are calm, we will work on their breathing techniques. Let's work on our breathing since it's something that can help us when we're feeling extremely angry and need to provide them with an alternate form of communication. Let's get some practice.

The last recommendation is

When the situation calls for it, seek some assistance.

On occasion, I will refer to the several tiers of assistance available in this space. Do not be afraid to reach out to the professionals that are located in your community; these professionals include psychologists, Child Development specialists, behaviourists, counsellors, and social workers. If you or someone you know has some experience or skill sets that could be of assistance, do not hesitate to get in touch with these professionals. And it's not just that you're reading my book; this is why I'm doing them as part of my job: to encourage you to put good parenting at the top of your priority list when it comes to your parenting responsibilities. You don't have to go through this process by yourself. Reach out to others and get whatever assistance you need to put yourself in a situation where you can assist your kid. It is encouraging to learn that there are certain things within our power to genuinely do.

Chapter 6

Establishing confidence

Choosing to focus on this chapter today—how to instil confidence in a child—is. Okay, mate, I know you're accustomed to this by now, but I have to remind us of all of our responsibilities as parents. You already know that no matter what happens, you will always adore them. However, many there are, as a parent, your responsibility is to love your children. Is there any way I can make it brutally clear? That is crucial because all of the tactics and advice I provide you are just a form of manipulation.

If this is your main focus, then adore them. Despite everything, even if it's just because we love them, we want them to have a more outstanding experience, as well as the right to have joy and happiness in their own life, and in order to do so, they must first learn a few things. What if we could assist them in becoming more self-assured? Then remember that your goal isn't to make them more confident, but since you love them, you'd like to sing more confidently, right? Because their life becomes more rocking, and it also includes yours. But that's not the reason we're doing it. How do you raise a self-assured child? How do you boost? Do you nurture a confident child? How can you boost the confidence that your child has? I'm going to offer three steps.

So let's have a look at step number one.

Entrust your child/Ren with a task that is within their ability.

Your kid will develop a feeling of purpose and success when they are given age-appropriate responsibilities and duties to complete. Make sure you let them know how much you appreciate their efforts, even if the work they've done isn't flawless. Praise them for all of the things that they do well, and reassure them that over time and you will see they will be more skilled in a variety of things, including the tasks that they have to perform.

Children have a feeling of agency and control over their life when they are given tasks and jobs to complete. In addition, taking on some responsibility around the home, even if it's only a few chores, may go a long way toward fostering self-assurance and a strong mental fortitude, particularly in a time when the future is uncertain.

Foster an attitude of self-reliance

Kids often see a significant surge in their level of autonomy throughout their time in elementary school. When children reach the age when they are in middle school, many of them begin to spend time alone at home, walk to school by themselves, and assist with the care of younger siblings.

It is essential that you give your children the opportunity to become progressively more self-reliant. For example, you should encourage them to figure out how to communicate with their teachers about any issues on their own, organize their homework assignments, ensure that their soccer uniforms are packed and ready, and so on.

The practice of parenting, known as "helicoptering, "weakens children's capacities to handle challenges on their own and has a detrimental effect on their sense of self-worth. It robs them of their independence, as well.

When your children are confronted with difficulties, you should encourage them to advocate for themselves and evaluate the situation before you step in. Their level of autonomy, as well as their sense of pride in themselves, will increase as a direct result of your actions.

Refrain from putting down your child in any way.

When your kid acts inappropriately or does something that irritates you, it is important to remember to separate your child from the behaviour. Because you are a human being, it is natural for you to feel frustrated or even furious when your kid presses your buttons. It is totally natural for you to have these thoughts; nevertheless, you should not indulge in name-calling or disgrace your kid.

Instead, have respectful conversations with your kid. Don't holler. Remove any emotions from your method of discipline. The use of natural and logical consequences, as well as maintaining a nice and friendly tone of voice while speaking to your kid, is an effective method for achieving this goal.

Chapter 7

Children who don't like expressing their feelings

As parents, it is natural for us to be concerned about the health and well-being of our children. Their emotions serve as a window into their soul and reveal who they are at the most fundamental level. Their emotions can teach us a lot and are quite significant.

If we don't talk about how we're feeling with other people, it can be difficult to form meaningful connections with them.

So the question is, how can we encourage children, particularly the shyer ones, to talk about how they are feeling? Or, if you live with a kid who has decreased the amount of time they spend talking to you, what can you do to urge them to become more forthcoming?

We don't want to put any stress on them. We don't want to come off as overly dependent or as if we have "an agenda," either.

While some youngsters have a profound comprehension of their emotions and the ways in which they experience them in their bodies, others have very little insight into these topics. It is not caused for alarm if your child refuses to talk about their feelings or is unable to do so. This post will explore the various options available to you.

I also discuss other options for having conversations with them about their emotions, including the following:

Avoid the habit of always waiting for children to come to you.

This criterion differs greatly from kid to kid. When you make it evident that you are interested in having a discussion, certain children will open up to you, while other children will only talk to you if they come to you first. Children are less inclined to talk to us if they get the impression that we are needy, too attached, or that we have some sort of plan or expectation for them to fulfil.

Try to strike up a conversation with your kid every once in a while. Be inquisitive. Take an interest in the individual's life. Find and talk to them. Inquire about the status of the situation. Inquire about the challenging aspects. Suggest phrases such as "Tell me more" and "What else is going on?"

Please don't overlook how they are feeling.

Do not provide a response that includes the expressions "That is not such a huge issue," "You are just being dramatic/too sensitive," or "Your jessant attention." Avoid saying anything along these lines.

Exhibit some degree of sympathy. You may reply something along the lines of "It is quite understandable that you might feel that way" or "It seems as if you are not feeling well." Is that what you have in mind right now? Alternately, "Oh, I get what you mean."

Avoid becoming unduly worried.

Children will avoid discussing their emotions with you if they fear that doing so will cause you to feel uneasy or worry about them.

Maintain your composure and have faith in your capacity to handle challenging circumstances. Tell them, "I have complete faith that you will be able to make it through this." You have the option of asking them what they would do in the event that they find themselves "in over their heads." Say something to the effect of, "If you get stuck, you can come to me or go to __ for help."

Try not to take their emotions personally and avoid becoming defensive.

Even if a child is angry with you, you should wait to share your perspective until the child has finished expressing themselves before you weigh in. Don't get worked up about the fact that they didn't come to talk to you sooner (they came as soon as they could).

Take in every word that is said. Communicate to them what you have learned, even if it is a criticism directed toward you. After they have had a chance to express themselves thoroughly, children can then begin to listen to you.

Chapter 8

Not quite yet; it's still not too late

Is it too late for me to alter the way that I parent my kid, and if I do change it, will it truly work? In this last chapter, I will discuss how you can modify the way you parent, as well as why doing so gives your kid a far higher chance of displaying improved behaviour when compared to if you did not change the way, you parent. Here are a few steps on which I will advise on becoming the better parent you want to be before it's too late; however, it's never too late to alter your methods, so don't worry about missing out.

Step number one,

Make a decision on the project you want to focus on first.

When I talk to parents, one of the most common problems I see is that they are unsure of where to begin. But I believe it's really straightforward: you should begin with the things that put your kid in danger. These are the behaviours that put your kid or others in danger, either physically or emotionally. For example, if your child is physically injuring another person, damaging objects, or acting unsafely outside the house, these are behaviours that need to be addressed immediately. My experience is that if you try to alter everything at once, you're going to be quite dissatisfied. Not only is it an unachievable endeavour, but you're also going to alienate your child. I also think parents should confront the items that violate their beliefs and morals and that are unsafe for their children and others. Start there. Do we want to alter everything? Well, good luck; maybe we can. But I believe we want to start with the most perilous, risky stuff and then proceed forward.

Step number 2

Determine what you want to change.

I believe it's useful for parents to break the behaviour down into distinct parts and work on them one at a time. So if your child yells at you, start with the conduct you want to modify most. When you chat with him, you want to break everything down. Begin with, "Don't yell. That doesn't help fix the issue, and I'm angered by it. What do you think you could do differently the next time you become angry?" Even if your child may be unable to think of anything, provide some options and persuade him to select one choice. And then add, "All right, now the next time you're furious, instead of yelling, you'll simply go to your room."

So concentrate on the behaviour you want to alter most—then go on to the next one. Don't attempt to handle everything at once.

Step number 3

Clarify the Change

If you're going to modify a particular reaction to conduct, it could be good to sit down with your child and explain what that change is going to be. Be clear about what you're going to do. Your child may feel upset and irritated, but don't allow him to turn it into an argument or any form of dispute. Say, "I realize that it could be irritating, but this is how I want our home to be."

I will advise that you don't make any form of speech but keep your statements precise and targeted. Remember, speeches cut down on communication.

Step number 4.

Define the objective

I believe it's vital to explain your aims to your kids. You can start the conversation by saying, "I've noticed that when someone teases you a little, you get really upset, and you get yourself into trouble." Other possible statements include, "My goal is that you don't hurt other people by saying bad words," "My goal is that you don't steal money out of my wallet," "My goal is that you don't punch the wall," and "My goal is that you don't throw sand in kids' faces or bite them when you're playing in the I detest it because you are then punished, and it repeats itself the following day. So let's come up with a fresh strategy for you to use going forward to avoid more difficulty. What can you do in response to being teased? And devise a strategy for what he may do the next time.

It's crucial to understand that not everything you say will reach your child's ears in the desired manner. Therefore, even if your youngster seems perplexed when you speak to him—he can be irritated, anxious, or angry—just try to maintain your composure. Whatever it is, tell your youngster, "Let's just see how it works out first; it's not a democracy, so we have to all agree on it." But it's a method of problem-solving that, over time, will alter how he views his relationship with authority—and with you.

Step number 5

Handling Possibility

If you're worried that your child is likely to do something unpleasant or damaging, one of your alternatives is to control the possibilities he has. Let's imagine you have a teenager who continually receives speeding fines. He doesn't react to your attempts to urge him to take responsibility and drive more carefully. One of the things you may do is take away his automobile. When you do that, you're taking away the chance. It's similar to younger kids. If they show that they won't stop taking money out of your wallet, take away the possibility by installing a lock on your door or keeping your pocketbook in the trunk of your vehicle. Opportunity management is one of the easiest techniques for changing behaviour. In other words, if your daughter can't manage the mall without throwing tantrums, don't take her to the mall. If your kid is in a restaurant and he can't stop acting up, take him out of the restaurant. Once your kid reveals that he can't manage anything, remove the chance until he shows you that he can. Often, if your kid doesn't get the chance to accomplish something, it won't happen.

Step number 6

Don't Appeal to Your Child's Emotions

Bringing up your child's empathy by saying, "Do you know how it feels when you're rude to me?" or "How do you think your dad feels when you steal his pocket money?" However, youngsters, particularly teens, lack empathy for anybody. They just aren't in touch with their emotions. The equipment in the mind that controls empathy is not completely established, according to some. Whatever the cause, empathy is not a method that will persuade your child of anything. As a result, they lack empathy for ordinary events; thus, you can't rely on that method to modify their behaviour. You must instead work with their self-interest. If you want your kid to change anything, you must show him that altering will benefit him; that it is in his best interests. If you want your kid to quit lying or manipulating, you must frame the situation in such a manner that he can understand how ceasing that behaviour will benefit him. "Can't you see how much your manipulation affects me?" isn't helpful. "Aren't you tired of being grounded for manipulating?" When you manipulate, you are the one who suffers. Remember, Josh, the repercussions will continue until the manipulation ceases. So quit torturing yourself."

And lastly,

Set boundaries and provide consequences.

I believe that understanding how to establish boundaries for our children is a key component of educating them. That's what your repercussions should accomplish. As a result, we cannot force our kids to change. However, by using the appropriate balance of consequences and incentives, we may make people ravenous for change.

Remember that consequences are only a means to an aim. And if you discover an effective result, keep using it. By "effective," I mean that your youngster reacts to it, even if only briefly. If the result does not seem to be functioning, it is not always necessary to go for a larger hammer. Always have a larger hammer in your toolbox, but use it gently.

Here's the deal: your kid will change eventually, if not for you, then for his employer, a court, his probation officer, or his girlfriend. Hopefully, he'll change before he does too much damage to himself. In any case, you're on duty now, and it's your watch, so just do your best.

So, how can you know whether your parenting style should be altered? If what you've been doing has been unsuccessful, I feel you need to modify your parenting style.

Remember, it is never too late.

Conclusion

The wonderful news is that while parenting is challenging, it is also tremendously rewarding. The unfortunate thing is the benefits generally arrive much later than the hard labour. But if we strive our best today, we will ultimately enjoy the fruits and have nothing to regret.

I wish all parents out there reading this book success.

To successful parenting!

www.ingramcontent.com/pod-product-compliance
Lightning Source LLC
LaVergne TN
LVHW050346160826
845677LV00014B/3817

9798366145244